The Bridge

Yvon Ledoux

Copyright © 2014 Yvon Ledoux.

All rights reserved. No part of this book may be reproduced, stored, or transmitted by any means—whether auditory, graphic, mechanical, or electronic—without written permission of both publisher and author, except in the case of brief excerpts used in critical articles and reviews. Unauthorized reproduction of any part of this work is illegal and is punishable by law.

ISBN: 978-1-4834-0038-9 (sc)
ISBN: 978-1-4834-0037-2 (e)

Because of the dynamic nature of the Internet, any web addresses or links contained in this book may have changed since publication and may no longer be valid. The views expressed in this work are solely those of the author and do not necessarily reflect the views of the publisher, and the publisher hereby disclaims any responsibility for them.

Any people depicted in stock imagery provided by Thinkstock are models, and such images are being used for illustrative purposes only.
Certain stock imagery © Thinkstock.

Lulu Publishing Services rev. date: 01/03/2014

This book is dedicated to my granddaughter Emma, born in Montreal, Canada April 17th 2012.

Acknowledgements

I want to thank first and foremost my Heavenly Father, who by His grace provided the inspiration for this writing. I also want to thank my wonderful wife who is my companion, steadfast supporter, and tireless encourager in the service to the Lord. The writing of this book was also made possible through my church family, and many dedicated servants of our Great God.

Contents

Introduction xi

Part 1: Living in the World 1

The Beginning: The Two Events That Would Mold My Life 3

The Second Event 7

This Is Not What I Was Expecting 8

Moving Far Away 10

Coming Back Home for a While 12

The Big Opportunity 13

England 15

The United States 18

South Carolina 20

The Point of No Return 22

A Last Chance 23

Finishing Well 25

Part 2: Living in the Word 27

Conclusion 77

Introduction

Before we begin, let's get a mindset of where we are going with this book. Is it spiritual? Is it religious? Is it just about a life that should have been, or is it about a life that could have been? Is it about a life that was granted success and filled with blessings, or is it about a life full of deceptions and sorrow? Is it about a life that spent more time walking under the bridge than on it? Is it simply one man's experience, or can many more relate to this story? The answer is probably "yes" to all of the above.

"*The Bridge*" is a simple book about a complicated life. What you are about to read explains why we should all connect our lives and daily actions with the Scriptures and desire an intimate relationship with God. Our relationship with the Creator is the bridge between our world and the one we can't see. It is the link between our every day life at work, our marriages, our families and the Creator of that world.

This writing is intended as an encouragement to others on their search for peace and happiness by discovering a God filled with love and with the answer for every question we face.

Part 1
Living in the World

The Beginning
The Two Events That Would Mold My Life

I was born April 15, 1945 and raised in a small town called Val D'or in the Canadian province of Quebec. Val D'or translated to English means *"Valley of Gold"*. The town got its name from the gold ore that was mined in this area. Life in this town was much like any mining town of that day.

Men came from far away cities to seek their fortune. Some stayed for a little while but could not take it for very long, as the work was extremely hard and dangerous. Most of the men who came originally were single and they were going from a gold town like this to the next one. Then women came to find husbands and hopefully form families. Children became an asset as soon as they were old enough to work to provide extra income for the household. Mining was the reason the town was built in the first place, so the other industries that followed were only there to provide service to the mining companies.

Mining was a difficult life. The hours were long and involved risking their lives daily. To deal with the stress, they also played hard after work and on the weekends. My father was a typical miner, a heavy drinker and a violent man when under the influence of alcohol. He often stopped by the local bar on the way home and spent a couple of hours drinking with his coworkers.

One night in particular after his usual drinking, he returned home in an especially bad mood. I was crying, as babies tend to do, and this made him very irritated. The more he yelled at me to stop crying, the more I cried. Then, in a fit of rage, he picked me up by one ear and threw me across the room. When I landed, I hit my eye and forehead on the kitchen table. My mom was terribly upset and feared I might die from the injuries. She rushed me out of the house and over to my godmother's house next door where she knew I would be safe.

I stayed there and was tended to by my godmother. The local doctor was concerned whether I would live or die. The impact to my head was serious and he was concerned that I might be crippled or disabled or have permanent brain damage.

As I recovered, my mother and godmother consulted with the priest about the best way to handle the situation with my dad's drinking. Knowing my dad's fiery temperament, my mother feared another incident would happen. After much soul-searching and discussion with the priest, my mother and godparents decided that I would not return home. I would live with my godparents and be raised as their own. Later, in my teen years when I was told of my adoption, I learned that this decision broke my mother's heart, but she felt it was the best thing for my safety. The couple that raised me for the first sixteen years of my life were actually my godmother and godfather. No one ever knew what happened to my birth mother. My godmother feared something tragic had happened to her.

My godmother came from Montreal, the Capital of the province of Quebec. Val d'or was my city of birth located 365 miles north of Montreal. Today this distance is driven easily in a day. However, in the middle of the twentieth century there were numerous single lane dirt roads that were considered dangerous. Nothing but forest existed for a hundred miles before lodging was found for the night and a place to buy gasoline when it was available. Vehicles were far from what they are today and broke down a lot, A journey in the winter could lead to death with temperature sometime reaching 40 degrees below zero and more. In the summer a traveler could look forward to spending some time with a forest full of black bears and wolves if the automobile proved unreliable.

My Dad was born in a village not far from Val D'or. His Father was a big 7 foot tall man who had spent his life in the forest hunting and living from the land. He passed away long before I was born but I had a strong picture of him from the incredible stories my Dad told me of his exploits.

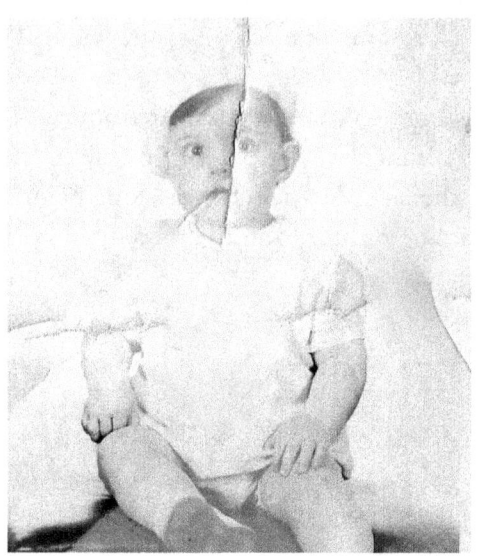

The only picture left of me in my parent's home after I moved out.

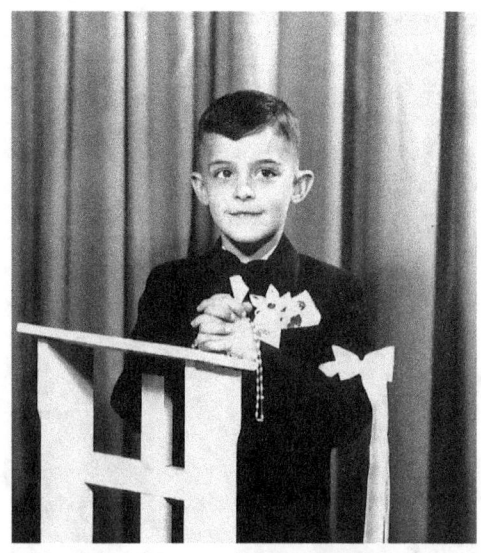

A picture after my first communion ceremony at 12 years old

The Second Event

One Sunday afternoon when I was about sixteen years old, our family had just come out of the worship service, and as was customary, everyone stepped outside on the lawn to talk with their friends and the priest. On that day, our priest happened to talk to my Mom and Dad. I was standing close enough to hear some of their conversation, but I wasn't paying attention to their words until the priest told my parents, *"your son, Yvon, will be a failure in life."* I was crushed, hurt, embarrassed and humiliated. I have never understood why he made this comment. I was a good student in school and did not get in any more trouble than the other children.

I had been taught as a child not to question authority, so to question our priest, the spiritual leader of our community, was unthinkable. So that day, and in days to follow, I decided also not to speak about his terrible statement again. However, like the athlete who trains for the Olympics with the expectation to win a Gold medal, my number one priority became proving the priest wrong. I determined that nothing or no one would stop me. Those nine brutal words would change my life for the next forty years. My determination would drive me to success, money, and the respect of my peers. But in the process, that same drive would take me to the verge of destruction and near-death.

This Is Not What I Was Expecting

Growing up in rural Canada, it was expected that as soon as a child was old enough, he would get a job and help support the rest of the family. My family was no different than most, we weren't wealthy and my contribution was sorely needed.

I set out in the world to get a man's job, like my Dad. At that time in the early 1960s, my father was working near a town called Chibougamau, Canada. I asked to join his crew and work with him at a logging camp. It required a time commitment of one year. My mother did not want me to go. She wanted me to stay in school. Against her wishes, I convinced my father to make me a part of his crew. In my mind, this was the first step in proving my self-worth to me and my family.

Back in that day, the distance we traveled to reach the lumber camp was more than 300 miles long and the roads paved with gravel. The roads were rough and some of them were single lane and filled with ruts. The journey would take over a day. Life was hard in the lumber camps. I was seventeen years old living and working among two hundred men all decades older than me. I went from a polite formal school environment to a raucous cacophony of lumber jacks telling racy stories using colorful language. Needless to say, I did not fit in at all. I was too young and inexperienced to participate in their conversations, and identify with their life stories.

The winter in the logging camp was terrible when the outside temperature would only reach minus 62 degrees during the middle of the day. Even though there was a man assigned to keep a big handmade stove heating twenty-four hours a day, most mornings when we woke, water in the big drums that we used to wash our hands and faces was frozen. The temperature inside the barracks where we slept was well below freezing point.

Much worse than the extreme cold of winter, the warm summers melted all the snow and transformed our working area into swampy land. The standing water was a perfect breeding ground for mosquitoes and biting black flies. These blood-thirsty pests were so numerous that swarms of them would appear as dark clouds producing a veil between your working partner and yourself. Summer season was the time of year we loaded all the logs harvested in the winter onto train boxcars. It was during July that my face and neck became infected from the insect bites I suffered at work. I was a young strong healthy man but the infection made me so weak I was unable to get out of bed. My father did not offer any help; he expected me to "tough it out and man up".

At the time I fell sick, I still had time to serve on my year's obligation, but the owner of the logging camp recognized how sick I was and told my father to take me home. The journey to Val d'or seemed like it would never end. When we reached home, my Mother could not believe what she saw. I was taken immediately to our family doctor who was in shock and thought I had leprosy. He had never seen anything like this and was greatly concerned. It took many weeks of treatments before I was able to take care of myself again.

Following that episode, all I wanted was to go back to school and get as far away as I could from the logging camp and the wretched life I lived there. Needless to say, my Mother was overjoyed with my decision to continue my education. Four years later, I graduated with an Electrical Engineering degree. That achievement was to become the foundation of my professional career.

Moving Far Away

After graduation, I was curious and excited to find out what life had in store for me. The only job opportunities in my hometown were in the mining and logging industry. So I found a job away in the neighboring province of Ontario, Canada. In the field of my study and what I had graduated for, it became valuable field experience that proved to be an asset later on.

This meant I would live some six hundred miles away from home. My new hometown was alive with people and vibrating with many large factories. Jobs were plentiful but unlike most of Canada, the only language spoken was English. Of course, I came from an area that spoke mainly French, but my best friend in grade school was a boy who only spoke English so I was quite fluent. Speaking another language was something that created an important opportunity for me.

I was facing the world for the first time on my own. To my surprise, speaking a different language was only the first of many differences I encountered in my new home. My traditional French upbringing made everything difficult. The mentality in the city was that if you came from an English background, you were superior. In my hometown, mining and logging management positions were held by English speaking people and the French speaking were employed in the lesser jobs. Again, even six hundred miles from where I started I was reminded that I was "less than" everyone else.

The next seven years provided a learning curve for me as well as many opportunities. I gained good work experience in those years that I worked in a few different manufacturing facilities. The goal of succeeding was at high priority for me. However, being young and immature, I often made wrong decisions. I made friends with people who believed that the only reason we are here on this earth is to get everything we can out of life. I had grown up in this small-town mentality where everyone knew everybody and knew everything about each other. Now, I was in the middle of a city a hundred times bigger and wilder, where rules did not seem important because nobody would know. All these beautiful teachings from my Mother about how to live in the way the Lord wants you to live, quickly faded away. They were not necessarily gone, but I convinced myself that could be overlooked for a while.

Although I knew I should have a closer relationship with God, I chose to ignore Him. I convinced myself that I had no time for Him. During this time I was exposed to people and things that drew me away from God into worldly bondages. I told myself that I'm young, and I'll consider my spiritual life later. With no one to guide me or correct me, my life followed a path of trial and error. Without realizing it, these experiences were shaping another phase of my life. Like the Israelites in the wilderness, I was lost, rebellious and soon would realize how much I needed God in my life.

Coming Back Home for a While

After seven years in Ontario, another major milestone in my life was about to take place--the decision to move back home. While I lived in the province of Ontario, I had developed a passion for Martial Arts and it became a major part of my life. Upon my return home, I formed a series of Martial Art schools in the region. One of my students, a professor of biology at a local college, became my good friend. I began taking classes there five nights a week to work toward a university degree in teaching. After obtaining that degree, I was offered and accepted a position as teacher in that college. Along this same time, I crossed paths with a young woman that I had dated in my teenager years. We fell in love and we were married a short time later. She had two lovely young daughters from her previous marriage and together we were blessed with our own child, another daughter, Isabelle. She now lives today in Montreal Canada and at the time of the writing of this book she had given birth to my granddaughter Emma.

Now one year later and in the final steps of improvement before publishing she will soon give birth to another beautiful girl. In fact by the time the book goes into print, I will most likely have the blessing of seeing her.

We spent the next twenty-seven years together raising the three girls. During this time, our life took many twists and turns that seemed at the time to be toward success. In retrospect I was going around and around in a worldly wilderness. My self esteem was always dependent on my achievements. Viewing myself as a failure was haunting me almost constantly; it never left me for very long.

The Big Opportunity

In 1976 a simple ad in a newspaper got my attention. The job it advertised seemed a perfect opportunity to move forward and fulfill my dream of becoming someone special. Convincing my wife to move our family from Northern Ontario for that new position was not easy. I managed to convince her by arguing that the income would be greater. We would be able to buy a better home, and the children would have more opportunities after being immersed in an English community and learning English as a second language.

For about seven years we enjoyed our new life and surroundings. My work involved manufacturing, heavy industrial mining processes, and projects for some of the largest paper mills in the country. At that time, the industrial world was moving towards automated and robotic process. Most everyone in the company that I worked for was hesitant to get involved with this new technology. I saw the innovation as exciting and challenging. I jumped in with all the energy and dedication I had. I knew this would involve a tremendous amount of time and study, but I saw this as an important development for the future of the industry.

It was in those seven years that my life changed dramatically. I started to feel like a success. A few years into this new challenge I was leading projects. My peers regarded me as a leader, a man of vision and an innovator in our field. I understood the worldly system I was living in, and as a result, I made the right business decisions at the right time. Many of my projects resulted in major gains and business success for the company.

My gift for innovation and thirst for new technology resulted in more exciting opportunities.

One day, a good friend and co-worker mentioned that he had seen a very unique automation graphical system in a steel mill he had visited. He did not understand how the system worked, but he knew I would be interested in looking at it. He was right. Within a few weeks, I was there on site investigating this new process. The automated graphical system I saw was so advanced and powerful that I couldn't imagine letting it slip through our hands. I saw our company taking advantage of this technology and getting into a market that did not even exist. From my work record, I was recognized by the upper management as someone who could move a project to another level. As a result, my boss gave me the go-ahead to acquire the technology for our company as my new project.

England

After my investigational trip, I made contact with the parent company that owned this new technology in England. One of their senior officers happened to be planning a business trip to the United States and agreed to extend his trip to meet with me in Canada. The meeting took place and as a result, my company started using the new technology in our production line. My intuition proved correct, this new process became a major standard in most of the manufacturing and process plants in our region, and my company led the way.

As a direct result of my work on this project, my company was awarded the *Queen of England Award* for imports in 1997. I was chosen from our company to take a two-week all-expenses paid trip to England and attend the banquet and award ceremony to receive the honor. This trip gave me an opportunity to spend some time with the leaders of the British supplier company. After that trip, my visits to England became more and more frequent.

One day the founder and CEO of that company asked me if I would consider working for his company. My answer was very simple and based on a little humor I said, "I have, but no one ever asked me." Shortly after that conversation I joined that company. My role was to head up a Canadian subsidiary as its CEO. My job was to put in place coast-to-coast Canadian distribution centers, to provide research and development for new products, and to supply the Canadian market. This necessitated Canadian software development and working closely with the parent company's team in England. Our goal was for the

Canadian operation to be profitable within two to three years. We achieved our goal by the beginning of the second year.

With all this job success, I once again remembered the statement made on that Sunday by our village priest, *"Your son will be a failure in life"*. I thought how I would like to see him and say, "See how I came out. I made it to the *big league* all on my own, by my hard work and dedication". All I could envision was a bright and uneventful future. There was no where else to go but up. I was in charge of my life, and obviously doing a good job with it, or so I thought. As the President of the Canadian company, I found myself away from home, frequently flying back and forth from Canada to England and all over the world. Along the way, I enjoyed big houses, new cars, and expensive boats. I bought anything my heart desired. Everyday I dined elaborately on the best cuisine and was entertained sumptuously by leaders of companies and industry moguls. Life was good, in fact, who would want anything more?

Just when I thought there was no limit to my success, I received a devastating phone call from our corporate office in the UK. It was 1997 and the founder and owner of the company had decided to sell out to a larger corporation. Some of the share holders in England, the US CEO and I offered to buy the company but it was too late. The papers had been signed.

To make things worse, three weeks later, my wife of twenty-seven years decided to leave me. All she could say was "I have lived for you all these years but you were never there. It is time to live for me." I could not comprehend how this could happen. I was in control and successful, but now everything was rapidly coming apart.

In the face of all these devastating circumstances, something in me snapped. My actions became completely irrational. I decided if I was going down, I would go down in high style. Since I had a considerable amount of money at my disposal, I found myself in a nice penthouse in an expensive trendy neighborhood. I had a life surrounded by everything a wealthy bachelor could afford. I pampered and soothed my wounds with whatever money could buy. Once a minor part of my lifestyle, casual social drinking turned into daily drunken binges. In an attempt to bury the pain, I was sinking slowly into a world of spiritual bondage.

The United States

For the next year and half, I lived in total rebellion from God. I was convinced that God did not love me, my wife and three children were gone from my life, and I felt nothing I did really mattered. One day out of the blue, I received a phone call from a company in the United States where I had worked in the past. They offered me a job as the head of research and development. There was nothing to hold me back. My work and my life in Canada were a failure; this appeared to be the perfect opportunity to get out of this slump.

The next two years were similar to my previous professional life. I was flying around the world on business this time in Scotland and Ireland. However, there was one difference. I was all by myself, my family gone, and I had little sense of what I was working toward.

I reached out to find friends in order to find meaning in my new life, but the fear of failure never left. In fact the friends I was seeking were the wrong kind again. My mind was in a spiral and the Lord was not even on the radar screen. In reality I did not even want to think about Him out of shame.

During the days, I worked as hard as I could toward success. At night I partied with equal fervor to overcome loneliness. In the end I realized that I had lost everything I really cared for--my family. The combination of working and partying at a breakneck speed and intensity was a recipe for disaster. I was always smart enough to drink at night but stop in time to be perfectly sober in the morning for work. One morning when I came to work, the President of the company, who had become a good friend came into my office and said, "Yvon, I have decided to sell 51% of my company". It was the last thing I expected but it was not the worst part. The same company that purchased our company in Canada and England was now purchasing this company. I was welcomed to continue working by management but I decided to move on a few months later.

South Carolina

Since I was already in the United States, I decided to take a job in South Carolina. The work was still high priority during the day, but partying after work began to take more and more importance. The years of hardly getting any news from my daughters broke my heart so much that I became extremely depressed. I could not perceive things to ever get any better. I had lost all hope. The village priest's statement played over and over in my mind. I was beginning to believe that the priest had been right all along. I reasoned that maybe he had an inside track with God that gave him this knowledge, all those many years ago. These thoughts and the alcohol abuse led to a severe depression. My life was sinking fast. Alcohol numbed the pain, and helped me escape reality. I thought of it as a shield that blotted out the ugliness of a world against me, at least temporarily.

For two months I had a long party enjoying everything I could buy or do. At times, it felt like I was close to happiness and then in a moment it would be gone. I was so depressed that I planned to take my life while on a trip to the Florida Keys. I spent hours on an isolated beach with a pistol in my hand, ready to pull the trigger, but I could not go through with it. It was as if a mysterious power prevented the action. All at once, I heard a still small voice within me say, *"It is not time. I am not done with you. I have a purpose for you"*.

I made my way back to South Carolina but nothing had changed. I worked all day and drank all night. One day after weeks of heavy drinking I ended up at the hospital. The doctor that cared for me told me, "you are doing a great job, keep on going and you will not be with us very long."

Following his recommendation, I admitted myself in an alcohol rehabilitation clinic. My counselor at the facility asked me what I wanted to do. My answer was, "I would just like to die, and I have nothing to live for anymore. I am no good to anyone. My family is gone." Hearing the desperation in my voice, he encouraged me to consider going to a place called the *Faith Home* in Greenwood SC. I told him that I had no interest in this place. From his description, it sounded like a God-centered rehabilitation program. By this time, I was convinced that God was not there for me. I had lost everything— my children, my family, my friends, even if I were to consider this, who would I do it for? I was tired of struggling. Still the counselor urged me, "What do you have to lose. It's only an eight week program. Give God a chance to speak to your heart." When I agreed to go, the counselor was so concerned that I would back out, that he convinced the *Faith Home* director to admit me right away.

The Point of No Return

From the minute I arrived at the *Faith Home*, I recognized that it was a very special place where God is at the center of everything. God is involved in every action, every decision, every day at *Faith Home*. Early in the program, I remember thinking they were all crazy there. Everything they talked about was "Jesus this…" and "Jesus that……" As matter of fact, Jesus was all they talked about. As strange as this was to me, I followed through to the end of my commitment. I went through the eight-week program, and to my surprise a few days before graduation, I was asked to consider staying on as Faith Home staff for a year. I accepted, and a short time later the Lord took my "mess of a life" and changed it forever.

One morning at 4 am I felt the need to go down to the chapel and pray. My prayer went like this: *"Lord, You know that one day I will leave here. I do not have the willpower or the strength to fight the demon of alcohol. It is far stronger then I am and I beg of You to take it away from me. I make a covenant with You that I will never touch even a thimble of alcohol the rest of my life."* After my time of prayer, I did not feel much different in my body, but in my spirit, I had a great sense of peace and relief.

A Last Chance

In the following year, I began to realize that healing had begun after that early morning meeting with God in the chapel. It was gradual, but the temptation of drinking alcohol has never bothered me since that day. It is a miracle of which I cannot take credit. The bondage was broken by the power of God.

Faith Home was my home while on staff for a year and a half. Near the end of my stay, I felt a call to enroll in a seminary class. As I continued studying the Word of God, and seek His will more and more, I realized everything He had saved me from. I learned that I have a special role to play in His kingdom. I was not so sure, however, that falling in love again or getting remarried was in God's plans for me. This seemed like the least likely thing I would ever consider. To my surprise, I met a wonderful woman, Diane, at seminary school where we were fellow students. Diane and I were married Aug 20, 2004. She is my perfect help-mate and the love of my life.

At the writing of this book, my wife and I have been married nine wonderful years. During those years our faith and constant striving to follow the Lord's guidance in our lives, has lead to many changes. Our life together from the beginning has always been surrounded by the Word of God. Our going to Church and our conversations everyday involve God and His will for us. Two years after we were married, I began to pray more and more every day. I would talk to the Lord constantly and speak to Him while driving as though he was in the passenger seat. I just felt the need and found comfort in it. The Lord would speak to my heart often and reveal things to me with confirmation so real that it would be impossible to ignore.

Then the Lord gave me this unquenchable thirst to study deeper and deeper, to seek Him and discover Him. I began to read books about Him and read His Word. I would and still talk to the Lord hundreds of times a day. He has since given me clear direction on my assignment for His will.

Finishing Well

During the last nine years prior to the writing of this book, I turned to God and His Will for my life and my family despite some periods of trials and rough roads. Life can take us to places we would never expect. Destiny is often referred to as something out of our reach, something we have no control over. We do not have control over everything, but God gave us the power of choice. Decision by decision we choose our path. Do we always make those right choices? I did not! Were they all bad? No. We so often hear or say to ourselves, "If I could start my life over again I would do things differently." We can say this all we want, but it will never happen. Do I regret some of the things I have done? Of course, however, I have repented to God and asked for His forgiveness. God in His great love has forgiven me. Forgiving myself and the ones who wronged me or hurt me was also necessary to truly be free from the past.

I have learned it is not how we start the race; it is how we finish it. It has not been easy, however, during these last few years. My obedience to Lord has led me into a ministry of caring for others. I author a daily devotional on the internet that is sent around the world carrying the message of God's love.

Diane decided to make a career change; she went back to school and became a Registered Nurse. Today anyone who knows her would say, she is exactly where God wants her to be. Her profession is her ministry. She has a heart for the people she cares for and their families.

My life began with the singular goal of capturing and owning my part of the world. But now my heart's desire is to finish the "race" well for the Father by doing His work on this earth. Together my wife and

I have found that putting God and His Word in the center of our life is the key to peace and happiness.

The Lord has spoken to my heart so vividly in the last six-month and virtually said to me, "You have not had this incredible life in vain, I have prepared you for your last assignment." My heart is full of love for His people and I submit myself to His will and will be obedient to what He will ask of me.

Part II

Living in the Word

When traveling on the interstate, consider how many bridges you go under in 50 miles. They are called overpasses, but they are still bridges joining two places. All would agree that the job of a bridge is to join things that are separated. God and His Word can be compared to a *bridge*. It is the *BRIDGE* in our lives from being lost to being a child of God.

The Pastor of our church always comments. *"when studying the Scriptures, we not only have to go deep, but we also must go wide"*. This is what we are going to do. One verse in the Bible may seem like something special, but we must look at the complete book to fully understand where the writer was going with it.

We are starting in Genesis, a good place to start, wouldn't you agree? It is the beginning of the Bible and a great place to start our devotions. As we begin, let us stop and define something of great importance. *Bereshith* is the original Hebrew word for, "*In the Beginning*".

Genesis 1:3-4 (ESV)
3 And God said, "Let there be light," and there was light. 4 And God saw that the light was good. And God separated the light from the darkness.

Through this word, we see God as the Creator of everything—the only One present in the beginning. We see Him separating things in order to make what would become the universe, light, and darkness. He made every part of our beautiful world, created the life forms within it, and eventually created you and me. We are so accustomed to all that surrounds us that we rarely ever really see it.

It's all a world created by God, a beautiful picture of the grace of God. In order to produce gold, rocks have to be separated. These rocks contain many different alloys, but at the end of the process, it is refined into gold. Metaphorically, we are all gold in God's eyes, but sometimes, we choose to remain in a primitive rock form. In the same way, a bridge can be seen as just a structure of metal and concrete between two points, but using our spiritual eyes, it can also be seen as something more. A Bridge is a link, a connection, a conduit, an association, a channel, and a passage.

At a very young age I worked in a gold mine. From my experiences, I will tell you that it was very rare to recognize or see gold as we looked through all the rock being extracted from the mine. Only after a long process and many steps did it become beautiful shiny gold in our eyes.

In Genesis, we have an earth that is not even close to what we know now. It was shapeless, formless, and void of life. Let's watch the first bridge being built.

Genesis 1:6-7 (HCSB)
6 Then God said, "Let there be an expanse between the waters, separating water from water."
7 So God made the expanse and separated the water under the expanse from the water above the expanse. And it was so.

I am sure you are wondering where I am going with this. Well, a bridge can be defined as a structure which allows passage across obstacles. It can also be seen as something which links pieces of music together.

To "*build bridges*" means to create an understanding between people or to try to make friends with someone who was previously an enemy. If you just eliminate all the physical bridges in the world right now, all of us would run out of food in a few days, run out of gas for our cars, and run out of many other necessary supplies.

In this passage, God has introduced the sky, the water and dry land. We just started to read the Bible, and we already are in need of a few bridges. As we continue in the Scriptures, let us stay in the mindset of gold being refined.

Genesis 1:8-9 (HCSB)
8 God called the expanse "sky." Evening came, and then morning: the second day.
9 Then God said, "Let the water under the sky be gathered into one place, and let the dry land appear." And it was so.

Now, we see God forming and shaping the place where man was going to live. He was creating a world of beauty and provision; He was creating a home for men to live in with all that was needed to be happy, where every need was met and every detail had been considered. He made it so that when man came to be, everything would be there so he could enjoy a life of abundance with God. Tell me that is not a work of a loving God. He was doing what a mom and dad do in preparation for a new child coming.

Genesis 1:9-10 (HCSB)
9 Then God said, "Let the water under the sky be gathered into one place, and let the dry land appear." And it was so.
10 God called the dry land "earth," and He called the gathering of the water "sea." And God saw that it was good.

Out of numerous things God has allowed me to experience in my lifetime, a while back I had the opportunity to walk on the Great Wall of China. This is one of the 'Wonders of the Ancient World', an extraordinary achievement built by men. We stand in front of things like this in amazement and awe, yet we fail to see the act of creation as a million times more impressive. In this moment, God was creating a masterpiece of beauty and provision, and He chose to put man in the middle of it.

In this scripture we see God filling up the pantry before He lets the kids come in, like the awesome Daddy He is. He makes sure that nothing is missing. And I ask you, how many people in the world today realize what the Bible is saying in this passage of scripture?

Genesis 1:3-4 (ESV)
3 And God said, "Let there be light," and there was light. 4 And God saw that the light was good. And God separated the light from the darkness.

Genesis 1:16-17 (HCSB)
16 God made the two great lights—the greater light to have dominion over the day and the lesser light to have dominion over the night—as well as the stars.
17 God placed them in the expanse of the sky to provide light on the earth.

There are two bridges seen in these few lines. Without light, nothing would grow on earth, and all that God created would soon die. This is the first bridge. Our great God, *The Light of the World* is the second bridge. He is on one side and we on the other. He shines, we grow. His loves stops shining upon us, and we wither and die.

Genesis 1:11 (HCSB)
11 Then God said, "Let the earth produce vegetation: seed-bearing plants, and fruit trees on the earth bearing fruit with seed in it, according to their kinds." And it was so.

Genesis 1:21-22 (HCSB)
21 So God created the large sea-creatures and every living creature that moves and swarms in the water, according to their kinds. [He also created] every winged bird according to its kind. And God saw that it was good.
22 So God blessed them, "Be fruitful, multiply, and fill the waters of the seas, and let the birds multiply on the earth."

God is filling the pantry again. He creates the sea and all the water creatures and adds more beauty to the earth creating birds. Again, we see a 'bridge of balance' here. Not one thing is left out. Before He introduces man on earth, He makes sure that every possible need will be met. He creates the perfect equilibrium for an earth that can sustain life. What do we see right from the start of Genesis? We see a God of love.

Genesis 1:26 (HCSB)
26 Then God said, "Let Us make man in Our image, according to Our likeness. They will rule the fish of the sea, the birds of the sky, the livestock, all the earth, and the creatures that crawl on the earth.

From Genesis, we can see that God always has a plan. We can see from the very beginning, God preparing the earth for a creature made in His own image, *man*.

My youngest daughter who lives in Canada, had been preparing for the coming of her first baby. She had decorated and stocked the nursery, buying baby clothes, and acquired the necessary supplies. In fact, she gave birth to a beautiful little girl just a few days after I started writing this book. She and her husband have been preparing in anticipation and love for the coming of this first baby.

In comparison, we see God preparing the earth for all of us with incredible love and anticipation, preparing a beautiful place for man to live with everything needed.

My daughter and her husband are a couple awaiting a life full of joy with their children. In Genesis, we see the Creator of the world awaiting a life of joy with His children. He has created a perfect connection, a *'perfect bridge'*.

Genesis 6:9-11 (HCSB)
9 These are the family records of Noah. Noah was a righteous man, blameless among his contemporaries; Noah walked with God.
10 And Noah fathered three sons: Shem, Ham, and Japheth.

11 Now the earth was corrupt in God's sight, and the earth was filled with violence

Just imagine God speaking to your heart and saying to you, "I want you to build a huge boat on dry land not even close to water." Now picture this, 'it will take you about a hundred years give or take a few years to do this'.

Think of your friends' reactions to your project. And mostly, think about the sacrifices you would have to make to be obedient to this request. There is no doubt about it; Noah was faced with many obstacles.

God never asks of you what you would expect Him to. He only asks of you what He created you to do. There is a big difference. The ultimate question that we see in Noah's story is, "are we willing to obey"?

Noah was chosen by God for this task. He was a man who loved God, and God had a special assignment for him to complete. The same holds true for each and every one of us. We all have a special part to play in the plan of the Almighty. God is working on the long term plan--not the short one. This statement is a negative message for a world that only sees in short term and believes that instant gratification is the way.

Everyone, I'm sure, has heard of this saying, "if it's not broke, don't fix it". I hate to tell you this; it is broken, and God wants you and me to help fix it.

Genesis 6:11-12 (HCSB)
11 Now the earth was corrupt in God's sight, and the earth was filled with violence.
12 God saw how corrupt the earth was, for all flesh had corrupted its way on the earth.

What I want us to realize today is that God is a God of details. He gave Noah the precise instructions on how He wanted the ark built. He did not say, "Noah build an ark big enough to accommodate every animal on earth plus your family." No, God was very specific.

Genesis 6:14-16 (HCSB)
14 "Make yourself an ark of gofer wood. Make rooms in the ark, and cover it with pitch inside and outside.
15 This is how you are to make it: The ark will be 450 feet long, 75 feet wide, and 45 feet high.
16 You are to make a roof, finishing [the sides of the ark] to within 18 inches [of the roof.] You are to put a door in the side of the ark. Make it with lower, middle, and upper [decks].

God is also very specific in every detail of all of our lives. Noah was connected to God, he loved Him. He listened and God spoke to his heart. There's the point! Noah was no different than you and me in God's eyes. The only difference is that Noah listened and obeyed.

Genesis 6:18 (HCSB)
18 But I will establish My covenant with you, and you will enter the ark with your sons, your wife, and your sons' wives.

'Covenant' is an important word used here for the first time in the Bible. Covenant is an agreement, a promise, or a pledge. Before there is an agreement made between one another, there has to be a link established, a connection made, or a bridge built. God has always wanted to connect with His people, to protect them and guide them to Himself. God could have saved Noah, his family and all the earthly animals from the flood a million other ways.

But, God chose the ark. God wanted Noah to build the means to get to the end result. God wants all of us to do the same. He wants us to get involved, to build the kingdom, to save the lost, and for our lives to be the means by which He receives the glory and honor! Now, do we see how important our daily behavior is?

We are building the Ark to Heaven. We are building the "Bridge to Heaven".

Man's wickedness comes from being disjointed with God. We can see this from the beginning of time, throughout every step of history until today. When we lose sight of God, we turn towards self. It's like the law of gravity. If the apple is not attached to the tree, it falls to the ground. If we disconnect from Jesus, we fall like the apple. Where do we fall? We fall into selfishness and self-focus.

Compare this image to that of a raised bridge across a river. For a ship to go by, the bridge must be raised. In this position, all traffic stops on both sides. What if you are stuck there facing that raised bridge for hours and hours? What would go through your mind?

There is one thing that we need to remember. We are in charge of our spiritual bridge; it NEVER needs to be raised where traffic cannot flow effortlessly. It always needs to stay connected to the other side.

We are building the Ark to Heaven. We are building the "Bridge to Heaven".

Genesis 15:18 (HCSB)
18 On that day the Lord made a covenant with Abram, saying, "I give this land to your offspring, from the brook of Egypt to the Euphrates River.

Hebrews 11:11-12 (NIV)
11 By faith Abraham, even though he was past age--and Sarah herself was barren--was enabled to become a father because he considered him faithful who had made the promise.
12 And so from this one man, and he as good as dead, came descendants as numerous as the stars in the sky and as countless as the sand on the seashore.

We come to another historical bridge in the person of Abraham. We see another covenant between God our Creator and man. The land and blessings are given to all of us through father Abraham. It is so important here to bridge this event of God speaking to Abraham. Centuries later Paul speaks to us in Hebrew 11:11-12 about the future of humanity.

What we must see from the start, from the beginning of time, is a loving God with a plan and that plan was not directed only at Abraham but to all of us even today. This applies to your life and my life every day. Everything He calls you to do has an impact on others.

Genesis 17:5-6 (HCSB)
5 Your name will no longer be Abram, but your name will be Abraham, for I will make you the father of many nations.
6 I will make you extremely fruitful and will make nations and kings come from you.

Again we see God speaking to Abraham. God was working on His plan of building all nations to come. What does this mean for you and me today? It means that the smallest detail with which God touches your heart may have less to do with you, and though you may never know why, they are part of God's big plan.

Kind words toward someone on the street could shake away that thought of suicide they've had for days. I dislike being so graphic but there is a hurting world out there and you may be the only one who can touch that person. That is why our every minute and every action counts. Be the light of Jesus every single day. Do not allow the excuses of, "I'll get to it later or tomorrow".

Genesis 22:1-2 (HCSB)
1 After these things God tested Abraham and said to him, "Abraham!"
"Here I am," he answered.
2 "Take your son," He said, "your only [son] Isaac, whom you love, go to the land of Moriah, and offer him there as a burnt offering on one of the mountains I will tell you about."

Sometimes we go through hard times. We question God, "what is going on in my life, why this, why that?" We have spiritual battles. God all along is saying, "trust Me, everything will be alright and obey what I ask of you." Aren't we glad He does not put us to a test like He did Abraham?

I know we are all saying, "But it's hard to always stay focused and be positive". It is difficult. Never forget He also said that He will never leave us or forsake us. Hang on to Jesus when life's difficulties come our way. From the beginning of the scriptures Jesus is already present as a B*ridge* to the Father.

Genesis 22:8 (HCSB)
Abraham answered, "God Himself will provide the lamb for the burnt offering, my son." Then the two of them walked on together.

Genesis 22:15-17 (HCSB)
15 Then the Angel of the Lord called to Abraham a second time from heaven

16 and said, "By Myself I have sworn, says the Lord: Because you have done this thing and have not withheld your only son,
17 I will indeed bless you and make your offspring as numerous as the stars in the sky and the sand on the seashore.

We see God commanding Abraham to offer his son Isaac as a sacrifice and then later providing a substitute for His Son. We see God speaking to Abraham that he will be the father of all nations. Then comes the perfect Lamb of God, Jesus Christ and His sacrifice in death for our sins.

That perfect bridge between the beginning of the bible in Genesis and the New Testament is our Savior coming. We can picture Jesus Christ in Genesis in the person of Abraham.

The bridge of redemption, in Exodus.
Exodus 3:8 (HCSB)
8 I have come down to rescue them from the power of the Egyptians and to bring them from that land to a good and spacious land, a land flowing with milk and honey—the territory of the Canaanites, Hittites, Amorites, Perizzites, Hivites, and Jebusites.

From Abraham's descendants in the book of Exodus, we see people in bondage and in slavery. At the present, 4000 years later mankind continues to be intoxicated with a life of self-satisfaction as a primary goal of life with little concern for others around them. God was concerned with the condition of His people, the Israelites in Egypt and provided a way of escape.

He is still working on the same project today. We need to shine like Jesus to show others the way.

1 Corinthians 10:4 (HCSB)
And all drank the same spiritual drink. For they drank from a spiritual rock that followed them, and that rock was Christ.

We see Jesus Christ as the Rock of Salvation, our Deliverer from sin. The same picture is seen in Exodus, when God's people were delivered from Egypt. It is so important that we see this historical event of the Old Testament being confirmed in one of Paul's messages. The message is that Jesus was always there from the beginning and He is the Savior of the lost world. *He was then and He is now.* Our steps and actions MUST be guided by the Unmovable Rock by our Ultimate Mentor. Setting the bar on Jesus, may mean we will never get there, but it also means we will never stop trying.

Exodus 17:6 (HCSB)
I am going to stand there in front of you on the rock at Horeb; when you hit the rock, water will come out of it and the people will drink." Moses did this in the sight of the elders of Israel.

1 Corinthians 10:4 (HCSB)
and all drank the same spiritual drink. For they drank from a spiritual rock that followed them, and that rock was Christ.

The Lord is our Rock, our Hope in times of battle against trouble, against sickness, against trials and hard times. Prayer is the answer, raising our hearts to God and seeking His help, comfort, and encouragement to fight the battle.

Exodus 17:11-12 (HCSB)
11 While Moses held up his hand, Israel prevailed, but whenever he put his hand down, Amalek prevailed.
12 When Moses' hands grew heavy, they took a stone and put [it] under him, and he sat down on it. Then Aaron and Hur supported his hands,

one on one side and one on the other so that his hands remained steady until the sun went down

We are to seek God to lead the battle, to fight the battle for us and to support each other in prayers. Aaron and Hur supported Moses' hands when he became weary. We are to provide the same support for each other in our prayers to fight the battles we go through.

Exodus 19:6 (HCSB)
and you will be My kingdom of priests and My holy nation. These are the words that you are to say to the Israelites.

Holiness, one of the greatest attributes of God, refers to His moral perfection. He calls His people (all of us) to follow a standard of ethical purity. Let's remember that God said He created man in His own image. This does not leave any room for any other standard but holiness. Holiness is submitting to the Will of God in our daily actions.

Leviticus 19:1-2 (HCSB)
1 The Lord spoke to Moses:
2 "Speak to the entire Israelite community and tell them: Be holy because I, the Lord your God, am holy.

A solid relationship exists between the Old and New Testament. The message God was giving back then is the same as He is still saying today. That's the *bridge*. One thing we must never forget, "God never changes". He is Holy, He is perfection, and He is the Creator of the universe. So the words spoken to Moses "*be holy because I, the Lord your God, am holy*" have the exact same meaning today.

I want you to say the following with me.......

The Lord spoke to (put your name here). S*peak to all your family, all your friends and everyone you care for, and even the ones you don't: and tell them* "*Be holy because your father in heaven is holy.*

Holiness seems to be something unapproachable, no use to try--can't get there. Some may say, "This is a God quality that is not for us". If these statements are true, why did God say that He *"created man in His own image"*?

Psalm 29:2 (HCSB)
Give the Lord the glory due His name; worship the Lord in the splendor of [His] holiness.

Our heavenly Father sent His only Son as a Redeemer, as the Way to reconcile us with Jesus, the perfect image of Holiness. Our goal every single day is to become more and more like Jesus. Why would we think that somehow God has changed His mind along the way? Are we so much smarter than the Israelites that the messages directed at them are not just as much for His people today? Jesus has stated *"follow me"*... Sounds like, "I am Holy so work on getting Holy". Can we master it? No, but if we work on it, we may start to look more like Him.

Exodus 19:6
And you will be my kingdom of priests, my holy nation.' This is the message you must give to the people of Israel."

God is saying *"My holy nation"*. God is saying this is the goal. This is, what "I" your God want you to do, anything short of this, is not good enough.

Exodus 19:6 (HCSB)
And you will be My kingdom of priests and My holy nation. These are the words that you are to say to the Israelites."

The world is moving so fast in terms of technology. Compare automobiles from 50 years ago to those of today. Society boasts mega structures, computers, telephones, and the list goes on. We call this progress, advancement, productivity. We're on the move. Let me ask a question. At what rate is the world moving forward in holiness? What is the difference between the guys in Exodus and the world of 2013?

Am I being negative or just realistic? You may say, "Man, we can't change the world, it's out of control." Jesus says follow me, do what I do. Sounds like a big job. Well, we have to start somewhere. A house is built one 2x4 and one nail at a time.

Numbers 14:18 (KJV)
The LORD is longsuffering, and of great mercy, forgiving iniquity and transgression, and by no means clearing the guilty, visiting the iniquity of the fathers upon the children unto the third and fourth generation.

We now look at the book of Numbers where we see a God of great mercy. 'Mercy', what a big word. I believe 'mercy' is one of the greatest words in the dictionary. Let us see the significance of that word today. When we look at a stranger or a co-worker, let us bring the following words to our heart: compassion, pity, clemency, forgiveness, kindness, sympathy, and understanding. They are all synonyms of mercy.

God was building His nation and God wanted to bless His people, the Israelites in spite of the fact that they were messing up. When we look at our world today, the ultimate goal of life appears to be self-gratification and self-satisfaction. Yet God has never and will never change. He is saying, "Come to me, I gave you the way, My Son Jesus". Why don't we understand that man's law is much harder than the Law of God? We never really think of it this way. When people come before a judge in a court of law sometimes the judge has a little mercy for a first offender. He will often say, if you come before me again the consequence will be much more severe.

When we look at our lives, and the repeated sins we have done against each other and our Creator, aren't we glad of the Lord's great mercy. A life of following the Lord is a life filled with forgiveness and mercy towards others. The evidence of this attitude is most recognizable in little things that we encounter every day. We respond to a remark directed toward us in an unkind manner. These are little things, everyday little things. We may not verbally say anything, but what comes up in our mind and heart in response to these everyday little things that we all face? I know what some are asking right now. How do we control our mind and heart responses? Quickly, think: "Jesus" and "Love".

Spiritual and Reality Bridge.
It is common as family and friends get together to bring up the past, to talk about memories and old times. Some of those memories are good and some more painful. It is necessary for us to look back at some of our life events periodically and rethink our direction.

Life is like flying an airplane. A perfect path of flight is only accomplished by a multitude of small corrections, not big ones. Likewise, fine-tuning our love for God demands constant small corrections in our daily life.

We often willfully try to erase all those bad memories or mistakes in our life. Looking at our past mistakes helps us correct the direction we are headed and avoid falling back in the same patterns.

Deuteronomy 7:9 (NIV)
9 Know therefore that the LORD your God is God; he is the faithful God, keeping his covenant of love to a thousand generations of those who love him and keep his commands.

God's love is so great that He keeps His covenant of love with mankind. He is merciful beyond understanding. God wants us to keep our covenant of love toward each other. Here is what I don't want us to miss: this means exercising love toward people who fail us. Here is the nugget: We fail Him every day and He does not stop loving us.

Mark 12:28-31 (NIV)
28 One of the teachers of the law came and heard them debating. Noticing that Jesus had given them a good answer, he asked him, "Of all the commandments, which is the most important?"
29 "The most important one," answered Jesus, "is this: 'Hear, O Israel, the Lord our God, the Lord is one.
30 Love the Lord your God with all your heart and with all your soul and with all your mind and with all your strength.'
31 The second is this: 'Love your neighbor as yourself.' There is no commandment greater than these."

We can worry every day that we are not following the Lord's teaching in a proper way. We can be outside God's law or outside what the Bible is teaching us. But the first commandment that we must always fall back on is what Jesus is telling us, "LOVE".

Christian is a big word too often taken lightly without thinking of the commitment that is required. Today couples get married with pre-nuptials of getting divorced. In other words, let's try this and if it doesn't work we'll try someone else. I have heard this statement many times, "I tried the Christian thing but it did not work for me." They prefer staying in the desert wandering for the rest of their life. Life does not have to be this way.

Joshua 24:15 (NIV)
15 But if serving the LORD seems undesirable to you, then choose for yourselves this day whom you will serve, whether the gods your forefathers

served beyond the River, or the gods of the Amorites, in whose land you are living. But as for me and my household, we will serve the LORD."

A hero of commitment to God was Joshua. I was not there with Joshua, but I am sure that he had to pick himself up daily and stay focused. He kept his eyes on God. The goal is obedience, commitment, finishing the race. Daily we need to part ways from our past and choose our new life with the Lord. Yes, it takes courage and faith to be consistent in our walk with Jesus. It is difficult day in and day out. Where do we get the strength? My answer is, 'from the One we need to follow, *Jesus.*' Where do body builders get their strength to workout daily? From commitment to their purpose, exercise, a healthy diet, supplements.

Life is all about decisions. When we really want something we apply the effort to attain it. We see this in the young athletes who prepare for the Olympics and in every human being who has set a goal for himself. This dream may be the reality of a new house, a trip to another country or a career goal. In order for these dreams to be achieved, there has to be a decision to make it happen. A plan has to be made. How important is it to us to accomplish what God has planned for each of us. Joshua realized that.

A *bridge* gets us across to the other side: so does a *decision.* Joshua made a decision when he said 'as for me and my household'. Joshua understood what God wanted from him. He knew the direction he must take. He needed to be an example and lead his family on the right path. Sadly, men often take a secondary role or no role at all in their family's spiritual life. They remark 'my wife is the spiritual one in our family'. Wrong answer! Men should stand strong in the Lord and lead their family in serving the Lord. Jesus came as a servant. He was obedient to the Father in His every detail. We as Christ followers cannot fall short of this pattern. The statement made by Joshua was strong, not questionable, not debatable, and not reversible. Joshua is not saying we're going to serve the Lord on Sunday. He is saying, "This is it, this is our way of life, every day".

Judges 2:10 (NIV)
10 After that whole generation had been gathered to their fathers, another generation grew up, who knew neither the LORD nor what he had done for Israel.

Judges 2:12 (ESV)
12 And they abandoned the Lord, the God of their fathers, who had brought them out of the land of Egypt. They went after other gods, from among the gods of the peoples who were around them, and bowed down to them. And they provoked the Lord to anger.

Another important bridge is in the book of Judges.
We see a God who is severe on one side and merciful on the other side in this great story. What can we learn from it? We see a connection bridge--our commitment to God and His dealing with us.

This is a sad picture of what happened then and is being repeated today--a nation that turns away from God to serve itself. God will not ignore sin. In fact He cannot tolerate sin and He will deal with it. He did then in ages past and will do it again.

A new generation that was not exposed directly to the events of the deliverance from Egypt had grown up. Although they knew about God's deliverance in the past, they did not experience it themselves. When we view things on TV versus seeing them directly with our own eyes it does not have the same impact. While I was in India and China I witnessed atrocities that still trouble me deeply today, and this was some 16 years ago.

We have seen reenactments of Jesus on the cross but we will never feel what people felt that day when they were at the foot of the cross. History keeps repeating itself with no change from the past. We have experienced great advances in medical technology that we did not think possible a decade ago. Yet we see a world in a spiritual dive that has not progressed in thousands of years.

When God's children cry out to Him, He is moved with pity, with mercy. He did it then in Judges and He will do it today.

Judges 2:16 (ESV)
16 Then the Lord raised up judges, who saved them out of the hand of those who plundered them.

Today we live in a world that is abandoning the Lord. Gideon, Jephthah and Samson were judges and instrumental in God's plan of deliverance of His people. Jesus came to deliver us from our sins, but also to take action in His plan. We could raise our hands in despair and say that we can't change the world. So we just give up? Or, do we say, "I can't change the world but I sure can make a difference".

Here is what we need to take away from this. We cannot expect God to isolate us from every situation. We are part of a nation, part of a segment of history in which there will be repercussions from the action that are taking place at this time. But the greatest part we must see is that we have *chosen* to follow Jesus. We are part of the winning team. The only worry we need to have is to convince others to join the winner's circle. God sent Jesus to deal with our sins and defeat the evil in our lives. Are we listening to Jesus?

1 Samuel 3:19 (NIV)
[19] The LORD was with Samuel as he grew up, and he let none of his words fall to the ground.

Life is a journey, with a beginning and an end. It can be compared to a race run on a track. It does not matter how we start but how we finish. The key to ending well is how we perform all the way along. If we read the story of Samuel, we see God's involvement in his life from the beginning.

God was and is involved in each of our lives but oftentimes we fail to realize it. He will use you and me to the extent of our willingness to serve Him. We live in a world of 'what can you do for me today' instead of praying 'God what do you want me to do today for You'.

Are we asking God to help us get to where we want to go or are we asking God to tell us where He wants us to go. The result will definitely be very different. Oftentimes, we hear people comment that they want to grow spiritually. If we eat everything God puts on our plate (even the broccoli), He will give us a larger plate. As pretty as roses are, they still have thorns so it is unthinkable to have a life made of a perfect dream. Growing demands effort but gives the greatest reward.

Samuel grew and he let *none* of God's words go unheeded. Talk about a heavy statement. *I am committed, I am serious, I have made a choice and I am going to stick with it, rain or shine.* We need to think on this statement. I am putting the accent on, *rain or shine*, I mean bad days--good days. Now let us take the Word of God in our lives and do not allow any to fall to the ground. This is the Jesus way and the right way. Now we are moving forward to Life in the Word.

1 Kings 3:12 (NIV)
12 I will do what you have asked. I will give you a wise and discerning heart, so that there will never have been anyone like you, nor will there ever be.

Wouldn't it be great to go to the pharmacy and buy a bottle of wisdom and vitamins and just take one a day? This is crazy talk you may say.

We live in a world of division just like in the Book of Kings. Good is on one side and evil on the other. Wisdom is needed everyday to discern even little things we sometime consider unimportant. King Solomon was given a special gift here in our scripture. Does it mean that because Solomon was given wisdom, it made him invulnerable from ever making mistakes? He was the wisest of men but he also made some unwise decisions in regards to his own direction later in life. Let's look at what follows.

1 Kings 3:14 (NIV)
14 And if you walk in my ways and obey my statutes and commands as David your father did, I will give you a long life."

The word *"if"* is encountered many times in the Scripture. "If" is conditional. God said, *"If you walk in my way"*.

Here is a problem we often don't realize. There is God's wisdom given to us by prayers and seeking the Will of our heavenly Father in our everyday life, and there is man's wisdom acquired through accumulated life experiences and what is defined as common sense. A great difference exists between the two. God's wisdom leads us to living in a way commended by the Lord. Man's wisdom can bring us major deceptions.

Go to the pharmacy and get a bottle of wisdom and take one every day. Wisdom that comes from God is nurtured every day. It is not a vaccine that lasts forever against a world full of deceptions. It is like a vitamin a day. To stay healthy spiritually and make wise decisions, take a trip to God's pharmacy. Imagine we are on vacation observing all the speed limits, red lights and other road signs. We will not get stopped by the highway patrol, or get in trouble, and will have a wonderful and pleasant trip. In other words, *obey the law*. What is God telling King Solomon? *Do as I am telling you and you will have all the blessing in the world.*

Now I ask a simple question, how do we know what He wants from us? We must ask Him!

2 Chronicles 6:41 (NIV)
41 "Now arise, O LORD God, and come to your resting place, you and the ark of your might. May your priests, O LORD God, be clothed with salvation, may your saints rejoice in your goodness.

The Ark of the Covenant. God instructed Moses on Mt Sinai during his 40-day stay on the mountain how the Ark was to be constructed. The Ark of the Covenant was a most holy vessel. Practically, God used the Ark as an indicator of when he wanted the nation to travel, and when to stop. Spiritually, the Ark was the manifestation of God's physical presence on earth (the shekhina). When God spoke with Moses in the Tent of Meeting in the desert, he did so from between the two Cherubs on the mercy seat. (Num 7:89).

Exodus 37:1-5 (The Message)$^{-5}$ Bezalel made the Chest using acacia wood: He made it three and three-quarters feet long and two and a quarter feet wide and deep. He covered it inside and out with a veneer of pure gold and made a molding of gold all around it. He cast four gold rings and attached them to its four feet, two rings on one side and two rings on the other. He made poles from acacia wood, covered them with a veneer of gold, and inserted the poles for carrying the Chest into the rings on the sides

The Ark was made of acacia wood overlaid with gold. Acacia is sometimes called iron wood because it is described as indestructible. Acacia wood symbolizes the incorruptible body of Jesus. The wood symbolizes humanity. Gold is used as a symbol of divinity. Jesus was not 50% man and 50% God as we seem to think. Jesus was 100% man, He was also 100% God.

The Ark "chest" contained:
1. Two Stone Tablets God's Law representing Christ the Living Word.
2. A Golden Pot of manna representing Christ the Bread of Life.
3. Aaron's rod depicting Christ's Resurrection.

Exodus 25:17-22 NIV
17 "Make an atonement cover of pure gold—two and a half cubits long and a cubit and a half wide.
18 And make two cherubim out of hammered gold at the ends of the cover.
19 Make one cherub on one end and the second cherub on the other; make the cherubim of one piece with the cover, at the two ends.
20 The cherubim are to have their wings spread upward, overshadowing the cover with them. The cherubim are to face each other, looking toward the cover.
21 Place the cover on top of the ark and put in the ark the tablets of the covenant law that I will give you.
22 There, above the cover between the two cherubim that are over the Ark of the Covenant law, I will meet with you and give you all my commands for the Israelites.

The cover or mercy seat rested upon the Ark of the Covenant and represents Jesus Christ the Seat of Grace, the Place of Grace, the PURPOSE, the Atonement. The Mercy seat was pure gold, notice--no wood. Gold represents deity. Here is the point, nothing but deity 100% God could save us and unite us with the Father. The blood of the sinless Lamb of God was sprinkled on the Mercy Seat. Note the top on the Ark of the Covenant was called the *MERCY SEAT*. They could have called it the *Forgiveness Seat*.

2 Chronicles 6:41 (NIV)
41 "Now arise, O LORD God, and come to your resting place, you and the ark of your might. May your priests, O LORD God, be clothed with salvation, may your saints rejoice in your goodness.

Now, let's put all this together in the second part of our verse. Please say the following…
    May your priest (Your Name here), O LORD God, be clothed with Salvation, may your saint (Your Name here) rejoice in your goodness.

I can hear questions. Are you implying we are all *priests*, that we are all *saints*? Yes, if you have your heart, mind and soul set on following Jesus. Hey! That was the goal then and it has not changed. In today's language it means for us to put on our "Salvation suit" and delight ourselves in the Lord.

A few years ago in 2009 my wife and I decided to build our dream house that I designed and built. In the great room there is a flat area over a stairway leading to the basement. That ledge was supposed to display something special one day. I could not imagine what should be placed atop this area even after it was completed. All I knew is that every time I looked at it, I was puzzled. Yet in my heart I felt it had to be something very special.

Well the answer came to me one night in a dream and at the time I considered this ridiculous. I was to build a full-scale replica of the *Ark of the Covenant* and place it on that ledge. You can see the *Ark of the Covenant* I built below. Since then, the Lord has impressed me to make the Ark of the Covenant available to churches to teach of God's love for us and His plan for our redemption.

Proverbs 1:23 (HCSB)
23 If you turn to my discipline, then I will pour out my spirit on you and teach you my words.

If we want to improve in any way in our daily life we need discipline and wisdom. This qualifies as easy to say but almost impossible for many of us to do. Can we all relate to this for a second? *We are going to* improve on something in our life one day. *We are going to* get in shape and begin an exercise program at the gym. *We are going to* visit a relative or friend more than in the past. *We are going to* call an elderly uncle once a month. *We are going to* read a few verses of Bible every day. There is only one problem with all these questions. The *"we are going to"* never gets done, or if it does, it does not stick around very long.

Discipline.
I watched the Olympic Games in London. It was so great to see the dedication and discipline every one of those young athletes had. All focus was on the Gold medals. In my opinion all of the athletes

were Gold medal winners by the discipline they exemplified as they performed and prepared for the Olympic Games.

Proverbs 2:6 (HCSB)
6 For the Lord gives wisdom; from His mouth come knowledge and understanding.

Proverbs 2:10 (HCSB)
10 For wisdom will enter your mind, and knowledge will delight your heart.

This may sound like a crazy illustration, but if you want to make a great cup of coffee, you first need to get great coffee beans!

How did Abraham, Moses, Paul, and everyone else in the Bible including the Most High, our Lord and Savior Jesus Christ, deal with all the issues, controversy and storms in their lives. They focused on the goal, the Father, the Creator and His will for them. How does one get the motivation, determination and discipline to make it to the Olympics? It starts with the dream to do everything needed to win that medal. Nothing will stop me. Nothing!

Proverbs 2:7-8 (NIV)
7 He holds victory in store for the upright, he is a shield to those whose walk is blameless,
8 for he guards the course of the just and protects the way of his faithful ones.

Discipline and determination are keys to attain a goal. Just as the athletes practice for the Olympics daily and not just once in a while, our preparation for the "Gold" has to be part of our daily life. How often do we hear, or better yet, have we said, "There is not enough time in a day. I cannot find time to pray or read the Scriptures daily." Here is the answer for all of us: Everyone on this planet has the same 24 hours a day. We don't find time. It's how we use it that makes the difference.

Proverbs 4:13 (NIV)
13 Hold on to instruction, do not let it go; guard it well, for it is your life.

The Word describes the "Bride of Christ" like a city having streets of gold. The Ark of the Covenant of the Lord was gold. The highest form of recognition and achievement to be attained at the Olympic Games is to receive the gold metal. This is God's standard. He did not make streets of silver or bronze. Our daily life and discipline need to reflect what God intended for every one of us. When we seek God's instruction on all we do He will make sure that His Gold medal awaits us.

Ecclesiastes 12:13 (NIV)
13 Now all has been heard; here is the conclusion of the matter: Fear God and keep his commandments, for this is the whole [duty] of man.

Everyone can look back at their life today and find mistakes. We have all heard or said to ourselves, "If I could only start over, I would do things differently."

Ecclesiastes 12:1 (NIV)
1 Remember your Creator in the days of your youth, before the days of trouble come and the years approach when you will say, "I find no pleasure in them"—

We can all benefit from this wise statement from King Solomon. We must realize that a life dedicated to the possessions of this world is empty without God at the center. We could name hundreds of things that can pull us away from God and the relationship we can have in Him. Man, since the beginning of time, has been in search of happiness especially since our senses control our direction. Natural man says, "If it looks good, and if it feels good, then it must be good." King Solomon, one of the wisest men to walk the earth, got trapped in this. The book of Ecclesiastes is proof of man's weakness. King Solomon was given wisdom and then failed to apply it to himself. He began to spiral down. What we need to see for ourselves in the Book of Ecclesiastes is a warning, not to be perceived as negative but constructive. If the wisest man known could fail, so can we.

Isaiah 35:8 (NIV) 8 And a highway will be there; it will be called the Way of Holiness. The unclean will not journey on it; it will be for those who walk in that Way; wicked fools will not go about on it.

There has to be millions of bridges in the world, wouldn't you agree? However there is only "One" bridge we need to pay close attention-- the One to Heaven. Isaiah said in the Old Testament there is a Way and He is coming....there is help on the way.... Jesus.

The Bible is not just to be read as a story of Abraham, Jacob, Moses, Isaiah, and many more. The Bible is the biography of many people in it. The failures and successes of the life of Abraham, Moses, and Isaiah and others are revealed. They were chosen, they had a task and they did it. What was Moses doing in the situations he was in? Was he obedient to God's direction for himself at that moment? When he was not, we see God intervening to change his course. Here's our mission. Let's find the Moses in ourselves, relate to our behavior and alter our course just as he did. You say I'm not Moses. No, but we have some of Moses in us.

It is not enough to just read the Scripture. We need to be part of it. We need to indentify with, to relate to the person we are reading about. The Word takes a new dimension. We now feel like we are part of it. What they experienced and what they felt in that situation we can identify. Does this mean to apply everyone and everything in the Bible? "Yes". If we want to be more like "Jesus" we must place ourselves in everything He did, everything He thought, everything He felt.

Think about this today, "What was Jesus doing on this day as He lived just over 2000 years ago."

Daniel 2:20-22 (NIV)
Praise be to the name of God for ever and ever; wisdom and power are his.
21 He changes times and seasons; he sets up kings and deposes them. He gives wisdom to the wise and knowledge to the discerning.
22 He reveals deep and hidden things; he knows what lies in darkness, and light dwells with him.

We want to hear the Word of God. We want to grow; we want to do our assignment from God. As we progress and learn every day, the Lord as He determines, will make us move up to another level. Oftentimes this is very disturbing. We feel disturbed, scared, wondering about what is going on and asking, "Why?" God is saying to us, "Don't worry. I know what is happening. It's OK! I've got your back."

Deuteronomy 29:29 (NIV)
The secret things belong to the LORD our God, but the things revealed belong to us and to our children forever, that we may follow all the words of this law.

God knows what lies in darkness. We don't. As we move closer and closer to Him, He speaks to our heart and reveals the deep and hidden things. At first we don't know what to think, we're confused, and want to react. We question, is this God? This is too much for me, and on we go. God is really saying, "Don't you know, I can do anything, and if I decide to do it through you, don't worry. I will carry you to the end. Just be obedient." "*I got it, says God, "and I got you.*"

James 5:7 (NIV)
7 Be patient, then, brothers, until the Lord's coming. See how the farmer waits for the land to yield its valuable crop and how patient he is for the autumn and spring rains.

Patience is in short supply today. We all want things now. We don't have time to wait, we are too busy. We apply this to God also. "Where are you Lord, in my situation? I would like an answer now." God reveals things to us when the time is right. He knows when we are in a position to understand them.

As the world is spinning faster around us, distractions come in from every direction. Frustration, panic, irrational decisions come from this pressure. So what should we do? This is the time to hit our spiritual rocking chair, exercise patience, apply prayers and God will provide the answer and direction. It is far from easy for you and me, but if we remain totally under

His wings and leadership He's going to do it for us. It's not us but Him in us who wins the victory. We physically can't move a mountain, but God can throw it across the galaxies. Patience is a big deal for us. Measure patience against eternity.

Hosea 3:1 (NIV)
The LORD said to me, "Go, show your love to your wife again, though she is loved by another and is an adulteress. Love her as the LORD loves the Israelites, though they turn to other gods and love the sacred raisin cakes."

The Book of Hosea is a story of a faithful husband and an adulterous wife and is an illustration of God's incredible, immeasurable love for all of us. In our willingness to grow we must realize that even with the greatest good intention we often times fall. Every day before us is a world of unending temptations. People get trapped in situations they did not even see coming. But, God is there with His open arms desiring to restore us.

The world is broken now as it was in the times of Hosea. Should this mean that in order to protect against evil we have to isolate ourselves from the world? No, that is impossible! We have to face the good and the bad recognizing the danger in front of us before it catches us by surprise. We are to daily seek shelter in the power and love of God. Wisdom and direction are found in the Lord before accidents happen. God's people have failed, and are still failing. Hosea's wife left him to be with her lovers, but God told Hosea to forgive her and show his love and to restore her. God is saying, "I have cleansed your sins by the power of the blood of my beloved son. I love you. Turn back to Me from what is unhealthy in your life and follow my spotless beloved son Jesus."

The everlasting love of the Father for each of us is the supreme example of love that has to become the objective in our own life. As we copy God's love in our every action the more it strengthens our immune system to failing our Lord. It is very difficult to relate to things we cannot measure. If we were given one gallon of gas, we could not drive very far, but if given a trillion gallons, we could say, we can drive forever. The amount of love we are capable of is like that one gallon of gas. God's love compares to the trillions to the power of trillions.

Water rises to the level of it source. If we tap into God's love at every opportunity, we can watch our love gage go up. We may even be able to get a bigger tank…

Amos 7:15 (NIV)
15 But the LORD took me from tending the flock and said to me, 'Go, prophesy to my people Israel.'

Amos is a wonderful book in the Old Testament--an attitude, changing book. Today's media, shows, and movies all have one thing in common. In fact they are all promoting the same image, a world with no fear, where the elite are dominant, the strong win and there is no room for weakness. This to many is overwhelming. This has such an impact on us that it carries to our spiritual lives.

We look up to the great pastors and we look up to the elders of our churches. They are great men/women of God. When we think of Abraham, Jacob, Moses and Isaiah we are awed by their stories and lives.

Then came Amos, a humble shepherd and fig grower. He was not a descendant of a prophet or high priest. In other words, he was simply a person like you and me. Now look at what God did through him.

The people of Israel were no longer adhering to their principles and values and had little devotion to the God of Israel. God instructed Amos to go to Samaria in the Northern kingdom and tell the people that He was going to judge Israel for their disobedience and sins.

We are so very important in God's plan just like Amos. There is a specific call from God on all of our lives. A task is intended for you and me that is for no one else to do. We must pray and get close to our loving Father. We must learn to recognize His voice. That is all He wants. Listen! His message to you and me will be clear and crisp and like a loving child, we must obey.

Amos 6:1 (NIV)
Woe to you who are complacent in Zion, and to you who feel secure on Mount Samaria, you notable men of the foremost nation, to whom the people of Israel come!

We have a world falling apart in every direction. There are neighborhoods in every city where people will not even drive through for fear of being attacked. Many people are in poverty beyond description and the world turns their head the other way. The general thinking is as long as I have everything I need, everything is all right. This is complacency.

There are people in need all around us with physical and spiritual needs. How will they know there is hope if no one tells them?

Amos 5:24 (NIV)
24 But let justice roll on like a river, righteousness like a never-failing stream!

This world is dominated by position, status and possessions. There is One to be feared, our Almighty God with all power and all dominion. He is Righteousness like a never-failing stream! God's love is never failing. Let us listen to God's call and obey it.

Micah 6:8 (NKJV)
He has shown you, O man, what is good; And what does the LORD require of you But to do justly, To love mercy, And to walk humbly with your God?

Taking orders, conforming to rules and regulations seems to be so difficult today. In a society where our uniqueness is the ticket to recognition, an immense challenge appears to remain humble. We try to separate our spiritual lives from our daily worldly obligations. The world has high demands. Some would even say it's a question of survival where the strong win.

Do we have a double standard? We act with compassion, love and humility on Sunday at church and on Monday we pick up our weapons to face the world. We can be strong, firm in our actions, yet act justly in love and humility toward others. What did Jesus do?

Every minute of the day, we come in contact with people. What do they need to see in our attitude? What do we say, what do we talk about? Is our conversation negative, pessimistic, defeatist? Or do we leave behind a feeling of hope, an optimistic point of view that conveys that we know Someone who is in control. We all have sad stories; this is part of being human. Do we nurture these bad experiences or do we focus on the positive and build each other up. It would be hard to convince a soldier to go to battle by saying, "Smile men; you will die today". Or would we say to him, "We are strong, better equipped. We have the ultimate team with God on our side and the battle is already won."

Love is what we must demonstrate everyday to everyone we meet. This is a love that can be heard in our conversation, seen on our face, and exhibited in our behavior which reflects a concern for our brother and sister. This WILL change the world. This IS reaching out to the world and our community. I believe with all my heart, that the most pleasing offering we can give our heavenly Father is for Him to see us display real *Jesus Love*.

Habakkuk 1:2-4 (NIV)
2 How long, O LORD, must I call for help, but you do not listen? Or cry out to you, "Violence!" but you do not save?
3 Why do you make me look at injustice? Why do you tolerate wrong? Destruction and violence are before me; there is strife, and conflict abounds.

Sometimes we would like to see the end of the movie before it actually ends. Or we would like the story to turn another way and have a different ending. There's a problem with that; we did not write the story. Life does not always go the way we plan. A job becomes more demanding then ever expected. Sickness and other trials come our way. Rest in assurance that life's story will end well when we place our trust in the Father.

As we live on, day by day, we tend to have a stationary look at things. Events come at us but not in the way we expect. Really, it would be nice to avoid them. Our friend Habakkuk was watching a dying world and it broke his heart. Many of us think the same way today. We "CAN" find peace in the middle of trials and chaos.

Habakkuk 2:3-4 (NIV)
3 For the revelation awaits an appointed time; it speaks of the end and will not prove false. Though it linger, wait for it; it will certainly come and will not delay.
4 "See, he is puffed up; his desires are not upright-- but the righteous will live by his faith--

We could look at the Bible as a great big movie script. The movie is 6000 years long from Genesis to Revelation. And here we are, all of us today a character of that great movie. Moses, David, and Paul had a lead role in that segment of the movie, but there were millions of others just like us back there with them. God loved them and wanted them to follow the path of righteousness. God never changes.

Habakkuk 3:19 (NIV)
19 The Sovereign LORD is my strength; he makes my feet like the feet of a deer, he enables me to go on the heights.

In the illustration of our 6000 years long movie, our great God wrote the script and the movie ends well... Gods wants us to play a great role in our section of the movie. This is where we have a choice. You and I may not be one of the lead actors like Moses or Paul but we can by choice, be an important supporting actor. We all remember the movie the *Ten Commandments,* not only a classic but also the greatest Biblical movie ever produced. I have watched it so many times and it is still so touching. Imagine now a movie of the Bible from Genesis to Revelation with all of us as actors in it. Our roles would involve being part of every book in the Bible from Genesis to Revelation. Here is God's question, "I have a great role for you to play in My story of the World, would you play it for me?"

Malachi 4:2 (NIV)
2 But for you who revere my name, the sun of righteousness will rise with healing in its wings. And you will go out and leap like calves released from the stall.

When we become sick, everything changes. A bad case of the flu and we are in bed. Being healthy is a big deal. When people get old, health is fragile and even the simple things get complicated. When the body becomes sick it needs healing. But what about our spirit? Can it become sick? Not only can the Spirit become sick, but it will also make the body sick. Our spirit can get sick when we allow ourselves to be influenced into seeking things of this world as the primary goal of our lives.

Malachi says that a healthy spirit brings a healthy body spreading to a healthy outlook on life. Our spirit can only be made healthy by our relationship with our God. A healthy spirit brings a healthy body, and like a stream of clear water, it flows to a healthy outlook on life. How does this work? How can I get a healthy spirit? The answer is in the beginning of our verse, "Revere my name". Revere means to worship and to hold in the highest regard. I like to call this priority, the highest priority. It all comes down to what we place as most important to us. God is instructing us very clearly, "Start every little thing you do with 'Me' your God, as number One. *Revere my name.* 'I' your God will provide you with a healthy spirit. *Righteousness will rise with healing in its wings."*

And lastly, when things are in that order, we can move on, ready to take on the world spiritually and physically. How can we face a challenge unless the mind and the heart are ready to conquer? When we have moments of stress we wonder how we will overcome this situation. The spirit is weak and we don't feel like putting up a fight. Spiritual strength only has one source, "God". It's all about order, *"for…*

you... who revere my name....will go out leaping like calves released from the stall." What a picture!

Matthew 13:9 (NKJV)
9 He who has ears to hear, let him hear!"

We have all heard these statements; *they hear what they want to hear, or they see what they want to see*. Another way to say this is, *as long as it goes in the direction I want it to go, this is the way I see it*, or that is the way I like to hear it. We cannot learn unless we are willing to learn. And our mind is closed to learning when we think we have all the answers. Growing in the Lord starts with humility and eagerness to learn.

Matthew 13:10-11 (NKJV)
10 And the disciples came and said to Him, "Why do You speak to them in parables?"
11 He answered and said to them, "Because it has been given to you to know the mysteries of the kingdom of heaven, but to them it has not been given.

This is my personal opinion. I believe Jesus spoke in parables because He knew we would get lazy and out of focus easily. Parables are part of the mysteries of the scriptures. They demand some effort in understanding them. The more we study the scripture the closer we get to God. And, the closer we get to God, the more He reveals and communicates to us through His Words.

In our scripture above we see the words *"given to you to know"*. The problem with all mankind is: *we assume, we got it, we know*. In fact if we pay attention in a casual conversation when someone tells us something, the first thing we say is, "I know, I know". God in His great love wants us to know. This understanding comes from the eyes and ears of our heart.

Matthew 13:12 (NKJV)
12 For whoever has, to him more will be given, and he will have abundance; but whoever does not have, even what he has will be taken away from him.

Coming to understand the scripture is through revelation and communication with our loving God. It is a great gift, a grace given by the Lord. This understanding is made available to grow the kingdom of God. When used accordingly more is given in abundance.

Matthew 13:15 (NKJV)
15 For the hearts of this people have grown dull. Their ears are hard of hearing, And their eyes they have closed, Lest they should see with their eyes and hear with their ears, Lest they should understand with their hearts and turn, So that I should heal them.'

The Lord wants us to know, and He wants us to get others to know about His great love. Jesus in His time of Ministry showed us a life that exemplified His love and obedience toward the Father and His love for everyone. The world is deaf to words. Our Christ-like attitude is sourced through the understanding of the Word of God and our relationship with Him. Our daily actions speak much louder than our words. The world will follow Jesus when they see Jesus in us.

Mark 4:21 (NKJV)
21 Also He said to them, "Is a lamp brought to be put under a basket or under a bed? Is it not to be set on a lampstand?

If we constantly thrive to fill our natural earthly needs, we can become too absorbed to hear what the Lord wants us to do. The *lamp* refers to the Christ-like witness in you and me. We must allow someone to see the light of Jesus in us each day. Just as the sun that shines on us every day and makes it easy to travel and work, God is the light of the world.

This light is channeled through us. To become brighter we must seek understanding in His Word.

James 1:25 (NIV)
25 But the man who looks intently into the perfect law that gives freedom, and continues to do this, not forgetting what he has heard, but doing it--he will be blessed in what he does.

James, Jesus' brother is very clear in saying, "Do not merely listen to the word..."

When we make every effort to obey and put into practice God's Word, our senses and understanding become more acute. We see clearer what the Lord means for us to do. He reveals more and more to us as we study His Word. He wants us to be responsible and deliberate in our commitment to Him. He really wants doers......

Mark 4:18-19 (NIV)
18 Still others, like seed sown among thorns, hear the word;
19 but the worries of this life, the deceitfulness of wealth and the desires for other things come in and choke the word, making it unfruitful.

The desires for security, prosperity, and no worries never lets go in our natural nature. This can become an obsession and shield the Word of God from being grounded in us. God always provides. He is the farmer. He disperses His seeds abundantly. Are we the soil He wants us to be?

Mark 4:20 (NIV)
20 Others, like seed sown on good soil, hear the word, accept it, and produce a crop--thirty, sixty or even a hundred times what was sown."

When we serve with a humble heart and enjoy our relationship with the Lord on a daily basis, we fall under God's will for our life. This daily communion with our heavenly Father leads to a healthy mind and a clear vision of the direction we need to go, shielded by the deceitfulness of the world.

Luke 19:8 (NASB)
8 Zaccheus stopped and said to the Lord, "Behold, Lord, half of my possessions I will give to the poor, and if I have defrauded anyone of anything, I will give back four times as much."

Things change when we meet Jesus. We must all realize that when the Lord touches our heart, there has to be a transfer of this to the outside. An action has to result from it. My Pastor said something special in one of his sermons, "We are not here only to do our time."

Zaccheus was admitting guilt, saying "I was doing people wrong but now I am going to change my ways". We all have done wrongs and being human we still do. This is about realizing it and doing something about it. In order to be obedient to the Lord, what changes do you and I need to make? The life of a Christian is the constant striving to be more like our awesome Savior.

Luke 24:45 (ESV)
45 Then he opened their minds to understand the Scriptures,

The Lord wants us to study His Word and the Holy Spirit is there to help us understand. We have all read a passage of scripture and found the message difficult to comprehend. This is normal. We ask other people, read other references, and consult our Pastor. But here is what we must never forget. Jesus said He would send the Holy Spirit to be with us. For understanding we must pray for the Holy Spirit to open our eyes, grant us understanding of His Word, and give us wisdom and guidance to follow God's intended will for each of us. And this is all laid out inside the Great Book.

John 6:27 (ESV)
27 Do not labor for the food that perishes, but for the food that endures to eternal life, which the Son of Man will give to you. For on him God the Father has set his seal."

Do we have the right motive? This is a question that should always be at the back of our mind. In our daily walk with the Lord our serving Him should always be motivated by love not by obligation. Do I buy a gift for someone's birthday because I have to or out of love for that person? The food of the Lord given to us is 100% pure love. This food brings peace, direction, clarifies uncertainties, and gives strength in moments of hardship. It is hard to see beyond the clouds when the storm is present but we must realize the sun is always there. The Son (Jesus Christ) is always there. The Comforter never lets us down.

Acts 1:8 (ESV)
8 But you will receive power when the Holy Spirit has come upon you, and you will be my witnesses in Jerusalem and in all Judea and Samaria, and to the end of the earth."

Telling the world about Jesus Christ and the grace of our loving God starts at home, our place of work, and our neighborhood. We have people all around us every day who do not understand who Jesus really is. Many still believe today that connecting with God and learning about His Word is something that is only done in church. The Pastor is there to fill that role and we the believers are there to listen and apply the Word of God to our lives. Yes, our Pastor is there to teach us but we are there to take the message outside the building. We are believers, and believers are mandated to spread the Word of God.

When we decided to follow Jesus Christ and make Him King of our lives, we were given the great gift of being inhabited by the Holy Spirit.

The Holy Spirit has become part of us. Therefore, witnessing to the world the greatness of our great God is our responsibility and service.

Romans 12:9-10 (NIV)
9 Love must be sincere. Hate what is evil; cling to what is good.
10 Be devoted to one another in brotherly love. Honor one another above yourselves.

At times we all need an adjustment in our sincerity level. We are like a car that has just been driven fifty thousand miles and needs a tune-up. Every day life has a way of teaching us short cuts. We feel the need to rush to the next task on our priority list. Love is expedited. It becomes routine, and non- intentional. It can also be pretended, so that we look good or we throw it in our big basket of "I need to get better at this".

No matter how we look at it, if we claim to have love for each other, it needs to be sincere. For this to happen we need to question our motives. What is the driving force behind our action? Am I being kind out of obligation, out of guilt, out of what people will think of me, or is it out of fear of hurting feelings? How can we improve if we don't know where our weaknesses lie?

Real sincere love comes at a cost. It demands effort, it demands concentration, and it demands determination and willingness. The little things that I do every day around me need to come out of a heart of Jesus that I reinforce every day by seeking His direction. Genuine love will not go unnoticed by the world around us. People feel it. It touches their inner core. Even the toughest hardest people (people who seem to have no emotion) are touched by sincere love. Sincere love is like sincere faith--nothing can stop it.

How do I get more of this sincere love? We get it from the One who had enough of it to send His Son to suffer and die on a cross for us.

We get it from Jesus Christ to make us right with the Father. We get it from the One who lives in our hearts, the Holy Spirit. God's love will never run out. We can't get a love anymore genuine than that.

And, He makes it so easily available. Go ahead, ask Him! But, be aware that He will send so much love we won't be able to contain it all. He wants us to go out in the world and give it away.

1 Corinthians 1:10 (ESV) I appeal to you, brothers, by the name of our Lord Jesus Christ, that all of you agree, and that there be no divisions among you, but that you be united in the same mind and the same judgment.

1 Corinthians 7:17 (ESV)
17 Only let each person lead the life that the Lord has assigned to him, and to which God has called him. This is my rule in all the churches.

Every one in the world has an assignment from God. Nothing is more important than this. We as believers have to make every effort we can to discover our specific assignment. We all have different roles to play as we go through life. Fulfilling this Will of God for our lives is the way to bring peace, stability and direction in our lives.

Galatians 6:1 (ESV)
Brothers, if anyone is caught in any transgression, you who are spiritual should restore him in a spirit of gentleness. Keep watch on yourself, lest you too be tempted.

We are all saved by the great mercy of our loving God. But this does not mean that we are to travel through life on our own. In other words when I am working on my problems, I talk to God. I read my Bible and seek direction. The Lord wants us not only in relationship with Him but also with each other. This means we are to seek help from others and give help to others in the spirit of Christ's love.

Ephesians 1:3-5 (ESV)
3 Blessed be the God and Father of our Lord Jesus Christ, who has blessed us in Christ with every spiritual blessing in the heavenly places,
4 even as he chose us in him before the foundation of the world, that we should be holy and blameless before him. In love
5 he predestined us for adoption as sons through Jesus Christ, according to the purpose of his will,

Before this world was ever created our loving Heavenly Father had decided that all believers would be adopted as His sons and daughters with all the privileges. He made this possible by sending His Only Son to redeem us from our sins. This alone should put a permanent smile on our face, and the greatest sense of peace in our heart. It's like this, it doesn't matter what happens, "I'm Daddy's little boy/girl."

This message from Paul is so powerful. When a family decides to adopt a child, this becomes a decision that will impact their lives forever. They bring this child into their home and give him/her all the love that they would a child of their own flesh. This is what God is doing with us.

Everything we do is based on measurement and a mathematical point of view: how fast, how strong, how long. We can even estimate that a creature is a million years old. But there is one thing man will never be able to measure, and that is, God's love.

Philippians 2:3-5 (NIV)
3 Do nothing out of selfish ambition or vain conceit, but in humility consider others better than yourselves. 5 Your attitude should be the same as that of Christ Jesus:

Selfish ambition can destroy anything. It can become a roadblock in our marriage, in our families and our churches. But when our efforts are tempered in humility the outcome has the opposite effect. Humility does not involve putting ourselves down. It requires being considerate, mindful, and aware of the needs of others all around us.

As we determine to become more like Jesus, we have to start wearing and embracing the same attribute of humility that He exhibited. The world views life differently where everything should revolve around ourselves and our success, regardless of what happens around us.

If everyone adopted the attitude of Jesus Christ, the world would become what it was intended to be in the beginning. Our world would be a place where people live in harmony and peace. There would no longer be war, crimes, and violence if everyone were content with what they possess and shared with their neighbors. The Lord has provided enough for everyone around the world to be happy. Man took over God's role and decided who deserves a lot and who gets a little or nothing at all. We see the results every day. Can the world become what it is supposed to be? It will when the Lord returns and makes it happen.

Colossians 2:8-11 (ESV)
8 See to it that no one takes you captive by philosophy and empty deceit,
  according to human tradition, according to the elemental spirits of the world,
  and not according to Christ.
9 For in him the whole fullness of deity dwells bodily,

It is easy to get confused and have mixed emotions about the direction we need to take at times. Traditions and ways adopted by the world lead us to believe we are to have faith on our human point of view. This will turn us away from following the Lord without our realizing it. Let us be vigilant as evil is all around us. It is so easy to get distracted by a world that is focused on doing what feels right instead of doing what is right. It takes but a moment of distraction to turn away from God.

Colossians 3:1-2 (ESV)
1 If then you have been raised with Christ, seek the things that are above, where Christ is, seated at the right hand of God.
2 Set your minds on things that are above, not on things that are on earth.

How can I live with a better Christ-minded attitude? We all go to work and perform the duties required of us every day. This does not prevent us from thinking about our family and all the ones we love. We make plans of all sorts. Let's invite our friends for supper, take the kids somewhere, etc. All these thoughts are part of our everyday routine. They do not disrupt anything. What we need to work toward, is to include things that are heavenly in our thinking process. Creating a habit only takes a few weeks of doing the same things consistently.

When we inject in our daily thinking process a mind of Jesus in every little thing, we are setting the tone for a behavior that will start to look and feel like Jesus. When we look at Jesus' life, we only see it as it pertains to specific events. It is difficult to comprehend that He lived like us one day at the time. He was 100% human and had to go through life the way we do. He had pains, ups and down, unexpected and unwanted situations, and He had to deal with it the way we do.

The important thing we must realize is that Jesus, above and beyond His daily responsibilities, always set His mind on the Will of the Father. He was about the Father's business.

Conclusion

In conclusion, "The Bridge" was written with two main purposes. Portions of my life story and its parallel in the Bible are to communicate that everyone's life can be visualized in every single book of the Bible. The Bible is the story of this world from the creation to the end. It is the story of what is to follow in eternity. It is the instrument of God's will for everyone's life. God's Word is the bridge from here to eternity. It is the bridge that will take us to Him at the end of our life here on this earth. It is my story and yours. It is where we are now and where we are going.

The second purpose of this book is to utilize the proceeds of the sale of this book to render help towards needy families in the community promoting the Gospel of Christ.

John 3:16 (NKJV)
16 For God so loved the world that He gave His only begotten Son, that whoever believes in Him should not perish but have everlasting life.

www.ingramcontent.com/pod-product-compliance
Lightning Source LLC
LaVergne TN
LVHW010558070526
838199LV00063BA/5011